ROLF ARMSTRONG

THE DREAM GIRLS

Ben Stevens

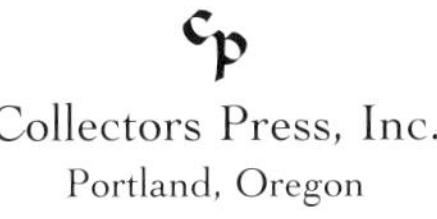
Collectors Press, Inc.
Portland, Oregon

Acknowledgements

The late Louise Armstrong; Duke Dayton; Dave Herbert; Dea Smith; Olga Steckler; Jerri Ruddy and most of all Jewel Flowers Evans.
Dedicated to the memory of Jon Evans.

Collection:
Ben Stevens

Photographer:
Fred Wilson

Editor:
Gail Manchur

Design:
Hoover H.Y. Li

Published by: Collectors Press, Inc.
P.O. Box 230986, Portland, OR 97281

Distributed by: P.E.I. International
Printed in Singapore

First American Edition

10 9 8 7 6 5 4 3 2 1

ISBN: 1-888054-03-4

NO POSTAGE
NECESSARY
IF MAILED
IN THE
UNITED STATES

BUSINESS REPLY MAIL

FIRST-CLASS MAIL PERMIT NO. 336 PORTLAND OR

POSTAGE WILL BE PAID BY ADDRESSEE

ORDER DEPARTMENT

Collectors Press, Inc.
P.O. Box 230986
Portland, OR 97281-9948

Rolf Armstrong

The "Dream Girl" as immortalized by Rolf Armstrong captured the very essence of the female form. Rolf Armstrong recreated the way Americans envisioned beautiful women. The "Victorian Girls," delicately rendered in pen, ink, and water colors by Harrison Fisher and Charles Gibson, had been in vogue as the "ideal" woman. A new look, a vivacious new girl, charming and greatly energized in brilliant colors, would claim her place and would be known as the "Armstrong Girl."

Rolf was born John Scott Armstrong on April 21, 1889, in Bay City, Michigan. His father, Richard, a Canadian by birth, owned a prosperous line of pleasure boats on the Great Lakes. His mother, Harriet, had Rolf late in her life and insured her maiden name, Scott, would continue with her newborn son. Young Armstrong had one sister, Chula, and two older brothers, William and Paul. His brother William had a son named Robert born the following year on November 20, 1890. So close in age, they were reared like brothers rather than uncle and nephew, and bonded for a lifetime.

In 1899 Richard Armstrong moved his family to Detroit, Michigan, and

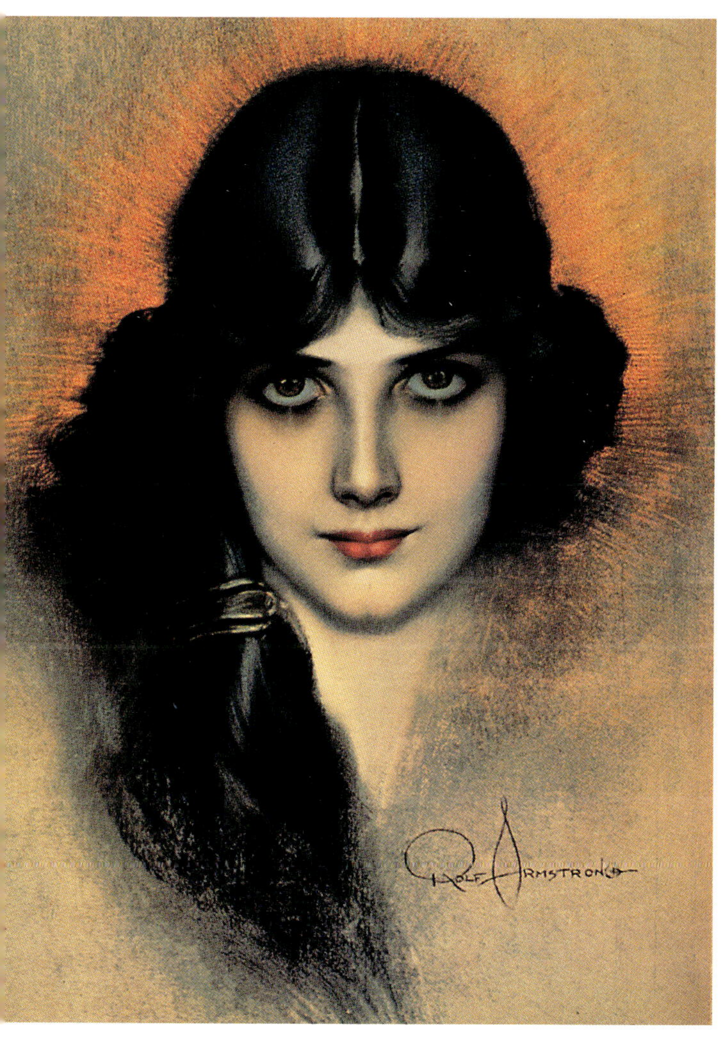
Rolf Armstrong

Judge Magazine "Live Wire"
Jan., 1912

shortly thereafter young Rolf's interest in art began to flourish. He began by sketching sailors, boxers, cowboys, and other macho-type characters. Then in 1903 Richard died when Rolf was just fourteen years old. The death of his father made him realize that he now faced the future on his own.

Armstrong's love of drawing continued throughout his early life, and his passion for art soon led him to Chicago and the renowned Art Institute of Chicago. There, under the

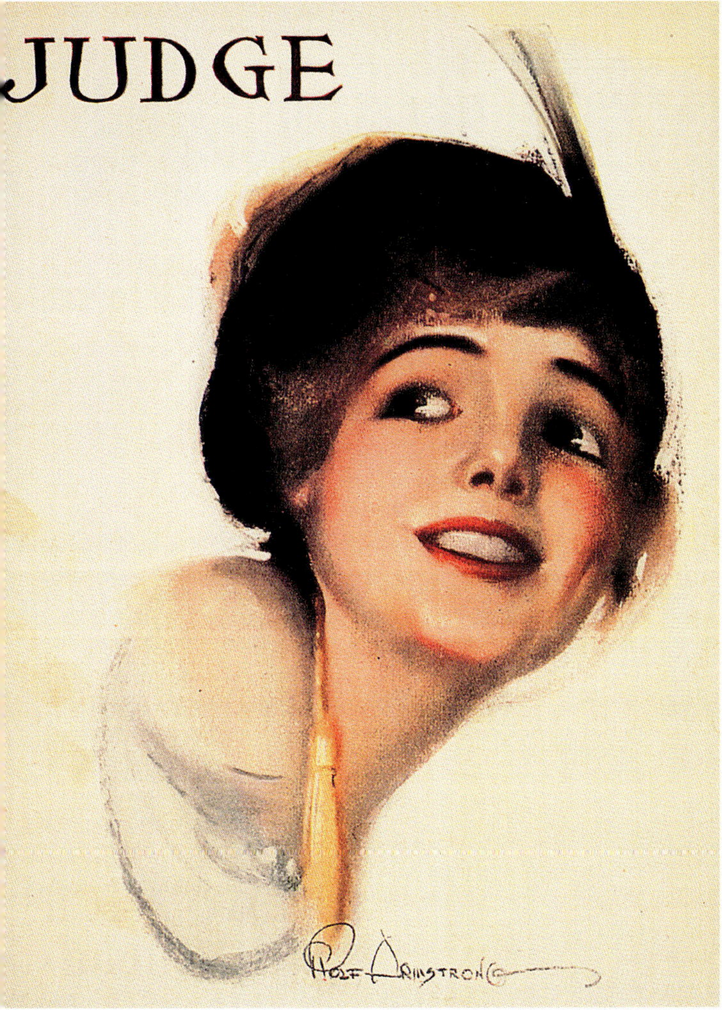
JUDGE
Rolf Armstrong

Sunday Magazine
Oct., 1915

skillful eye and expert tutelage of Master Draftsman John Vanderpoel, Rolf's long career in art began. While a student, John Scott adopted "Rolf" as his professional name. Soon his distinguished signature would become his famous, lifelong trademark.

Rolf struggled to survive during his student days in Chicago. To earn money, he taught boxing, baseball, and art, and took on any other job he could find. He roomed with three other men including Thomas Hart Benton, who

Boston Sunday Post

SUNDAY MAGAZINE

PART 5 BOSTON, MASS. OCTOBER 3, 1915 16 PAGES

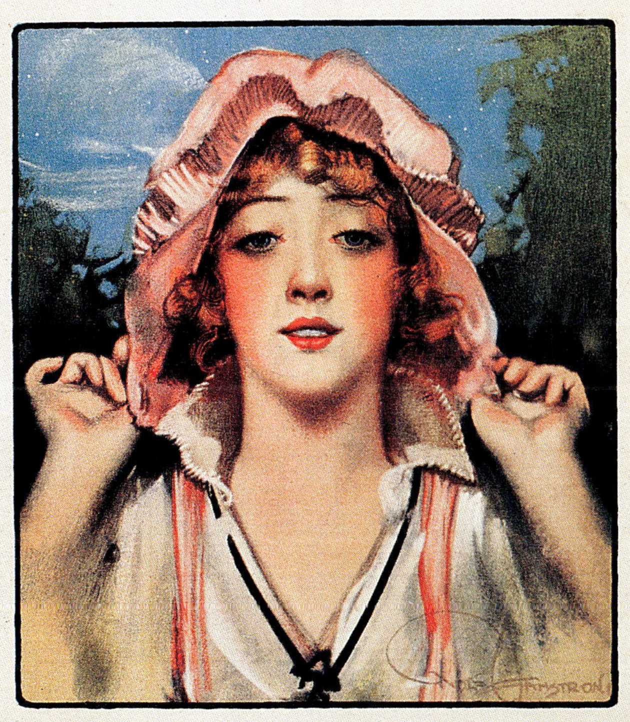

Metropolitan
July, 1913

would become famous for his epic murals depicting America's social history.

Like many of his fellow students, Rolf moved to New York City where the big magazines were well established and where he and Benton would meet again. This time they would struggle to survive in the Old Lincoln Arcade in Manhattan, which was infested with rats, fleas, and bedbugs. This ramshackle building was a gathering place for the poorest

METROPOLITAN

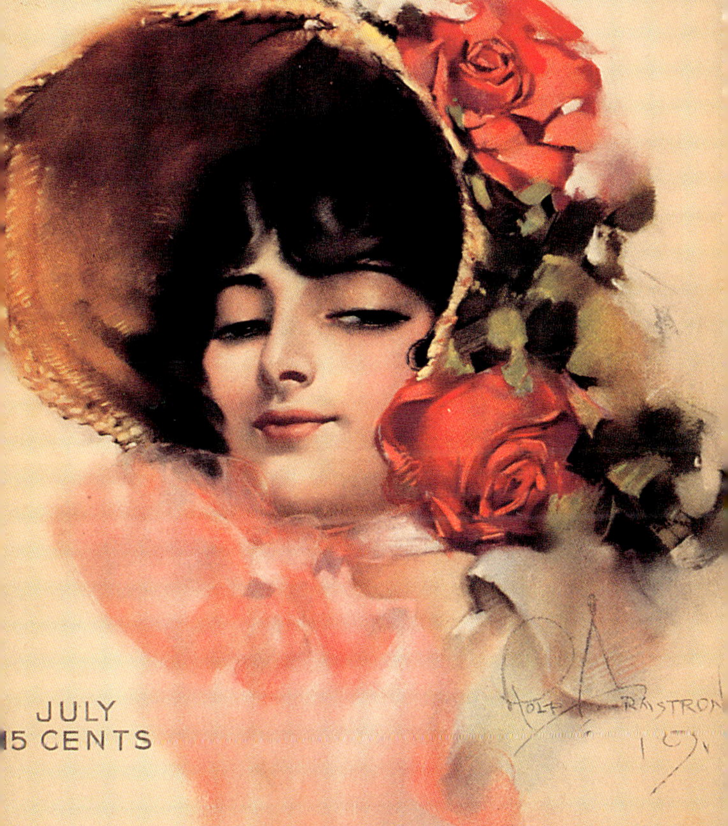

THE LIVEST MAGAZINE IN AMERICA

Puck "Foxy"
Jan., 1916

of New York's aspiring artists, writers, musicians, actors, athletes, and body builders.

Rolf soon began to prosper. He had been well prepared in Chicago to enter the profession of commercial illustrator and artist. His chosen subject of "feminine beauty" was now very popular, and he was very familiar with recent technological improvements in printing and the subsequent demand for brilliant colors in magazine illustrations. Rolf had

Puck

WEEK ENDING JANUARY 29, 191
PRICE TEN CENTS

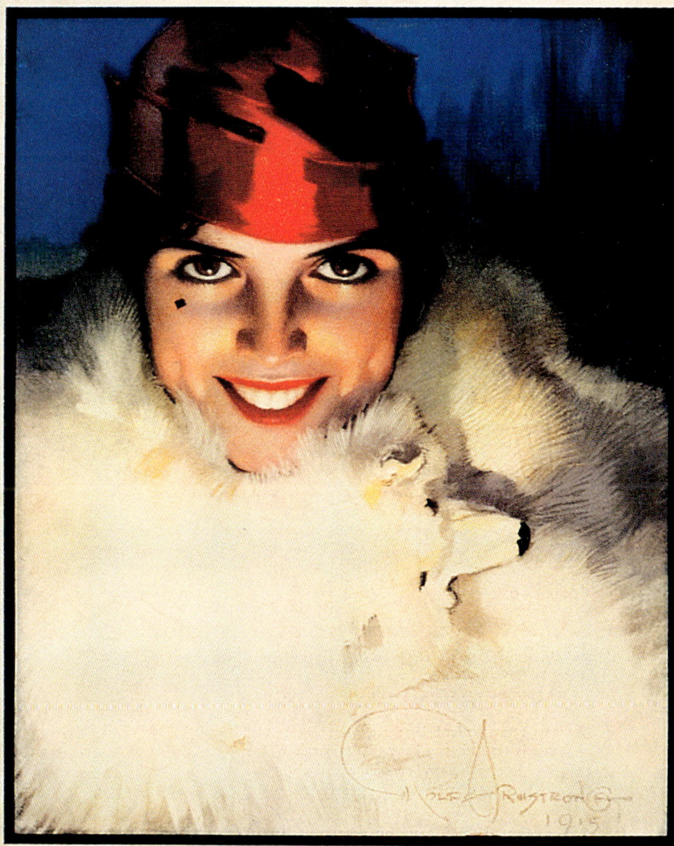

Painted by Rolf Armstrong

The Stewart Lever "Safety First"
Apr., 1916

perfected his skills with the seasoned artist's medium, pastels, those little chisel-edged crayons that came in an amazing assortment of brilliant colors. With his abundant talent, and perhaps fate on his side, his career was soon well launched.

By January, 1912 when he was only twenty-two, *Judge* magazine featured Rolf's "A Live Wire" on the cover, believed to be the first of the many magazine covers he produced. His first image must have been well

THE *Stewart* LEVER

APRIL 1916

TEN CENTS THE COPY

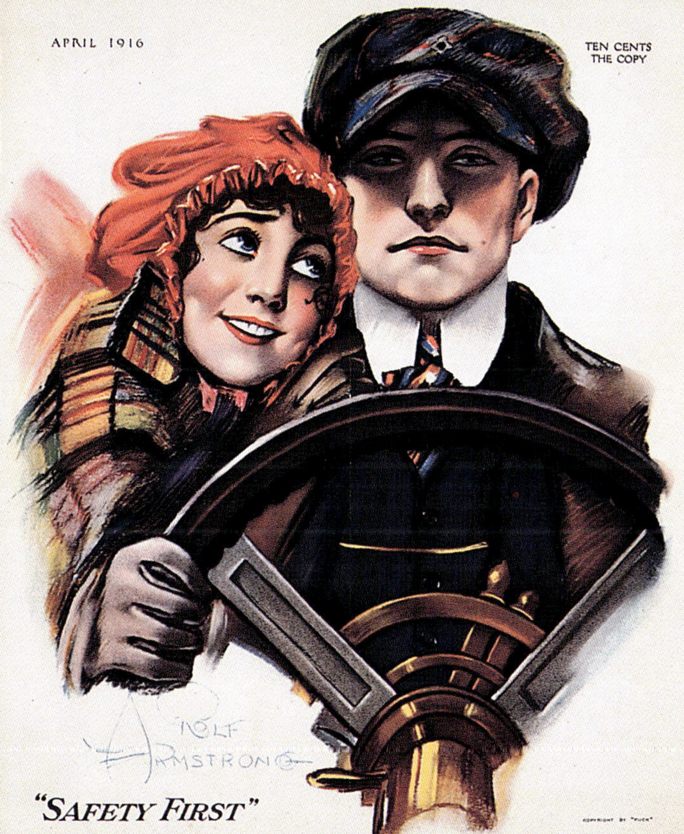

"SAFETY FIRST"

Published by Stewart-Warner Speedometer Corporation, Chicago

Circulation 100,000 copies.

The Stewart Lever
"A Mid-Summer Night's Dream"
1917

received for in the following June 22 issue, a bright eyed brunette, "Good For What Ails You!" made her debut. In November and in January, 1913 stunning portraits appeared on the covers of *American Sunday Magazine*, a tabloid published by The Associated Sunday Magazine, Incorporated as an insert for the *Chicago Examiner*. Perhaps the early recognition of Rolf's name and his very early success resulted from these Sunday tabloid inserts. They were included in many

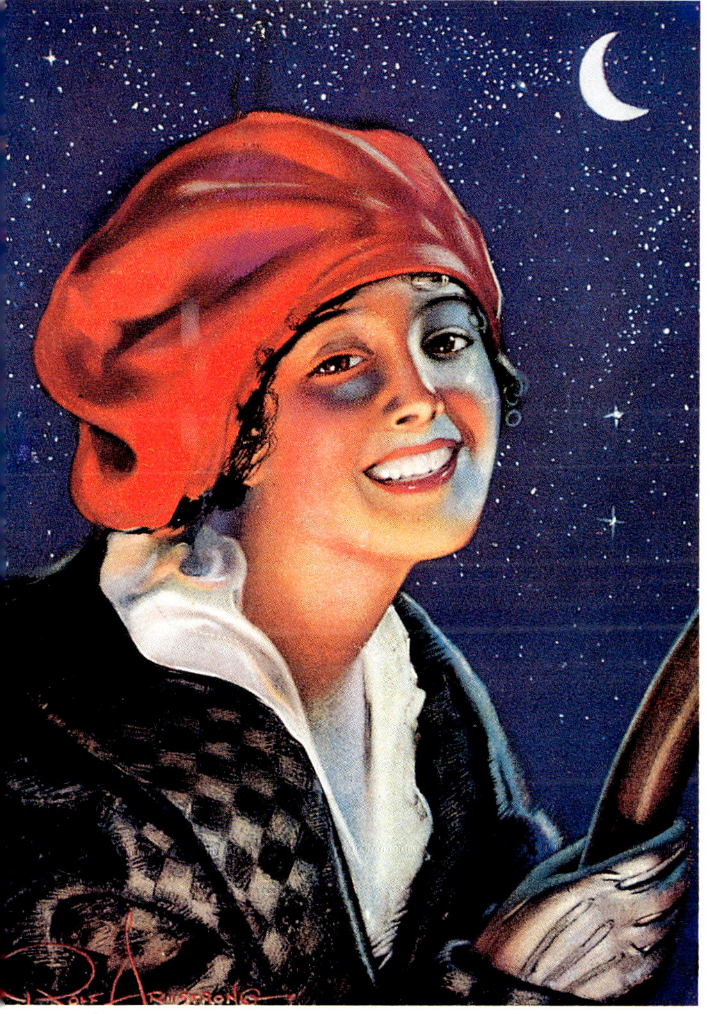
ROLF ARMSTRONG

Metropolitan
ca. 1917

of America's leading newspapers so millions of readers saw the new "Armstrong Girl." Soon magazine publishers and advertisers were clamoring for his work.

The "Armstrong Girls" appeared in Sunday newspaper tabloids, on magazine covers, sheet music, calendars, commercial advertising, post cards, and ink blotters. Rolf's first calendar girl, "Dream Girl," appeared in 1919. The title was used again and became associated with his great success.

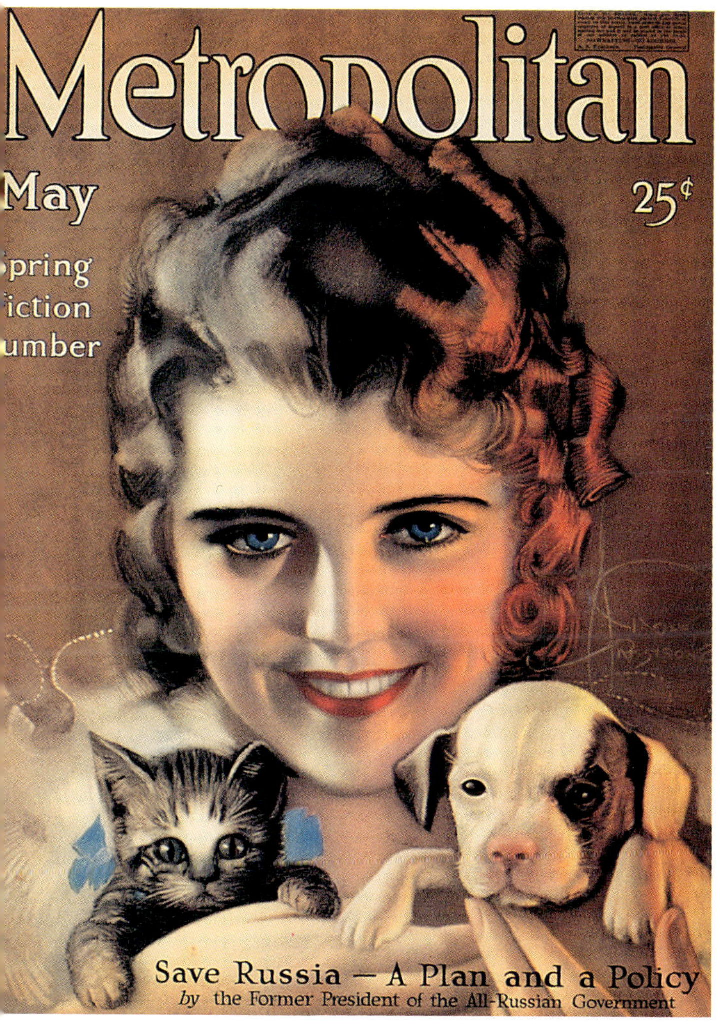
Metropolitan
May
25¢
Spring
Fiction
Number
Save Russia — A Plan and a Policy
by the Former President of the All-Russian Government

Metropolitan
ca. 1917

The Knapp Company, Incorporated, of New York, was one of Armstrong's clients and was instrumental in his early success. Rolf's images appeared and reappeared as Knapp utilized his work in many different applications. The same image used for calendars would also appear on ink blotters and post cards. In other applications, drawings from the cover of the prestigious *Metropolitan* magazine would also be used on sheet music and calendar prints. Knapp also

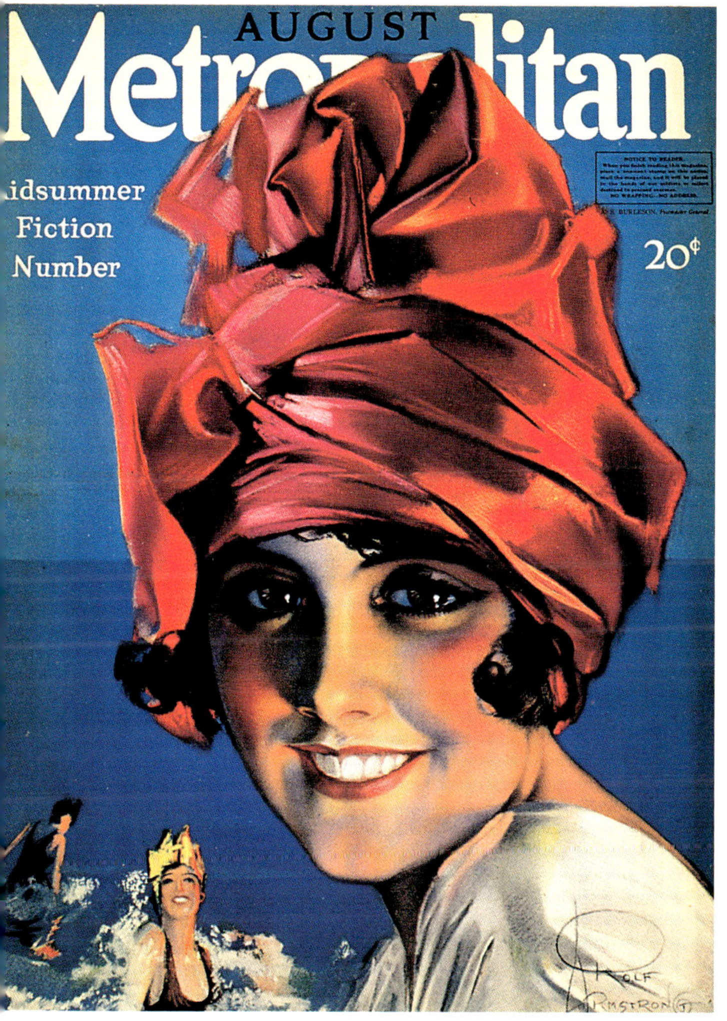
AUGUST
Metr
litan
idsummer
Fiction
Number
20¢

American Magazine
Oct., 1919

allowed the new "Armstrong Girls" to be featured on *Puck*, a political satire consumer publication, and on *The Stewart Lever*, an automotive trade publication. *The Stewart Lever* illustration, "Safety First" included a self-portrait of Rolf as the driver. Rolf's magazine clients soon included: *American Magazine*; *Colliers*; *The Delineator*; *McCalls*; *The People's Home Journal*; *Pictorial Review*; *The Saturday Evening Post*; *Woman's Home Companion*; and *Photoplay Magazine*, among others.

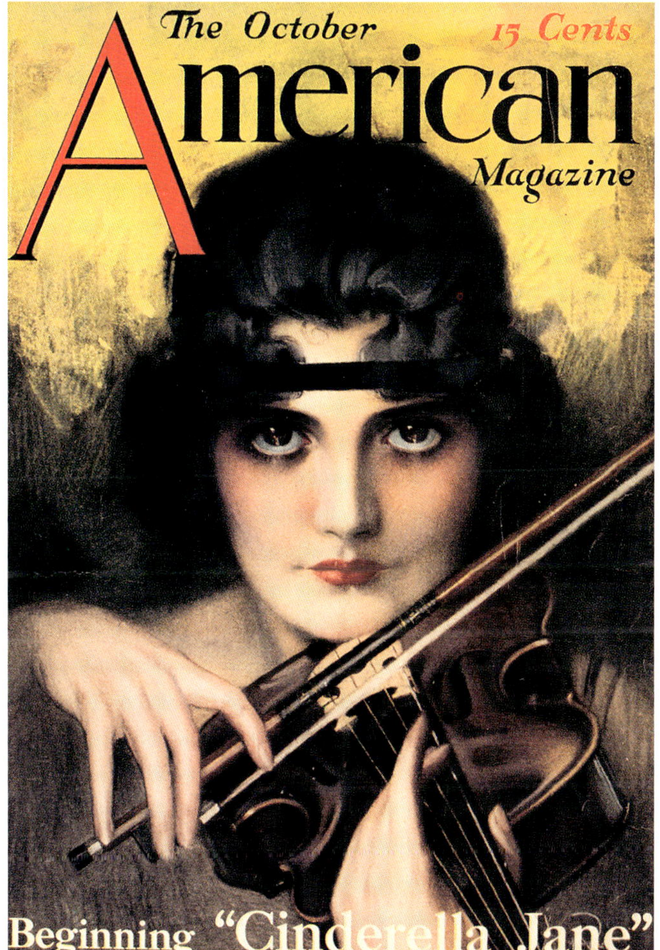
The October
15 Cents
American
Magazine
Beginning "Cinderella Jane"
A love story by the author of "Bamby"

Knapp Co. Sheet Music "Drifting"
1919

Rolf's brother Paul had moved to New York City to work as a playwright. His plays, *Salomy Jane*, *Deep Purple*, and *The Greyhound*, were successes, and his biggest hit was *Alias Jimmy Valentine*. Rolf enjoyed his brother's success and occasionally socialized within Paul's circle of friends where he met and was soon smitten by an aspiring young actress, Claire Louise Frisby.

In 1919 Rolf married Louise and they went to Paris. Rolf studied and

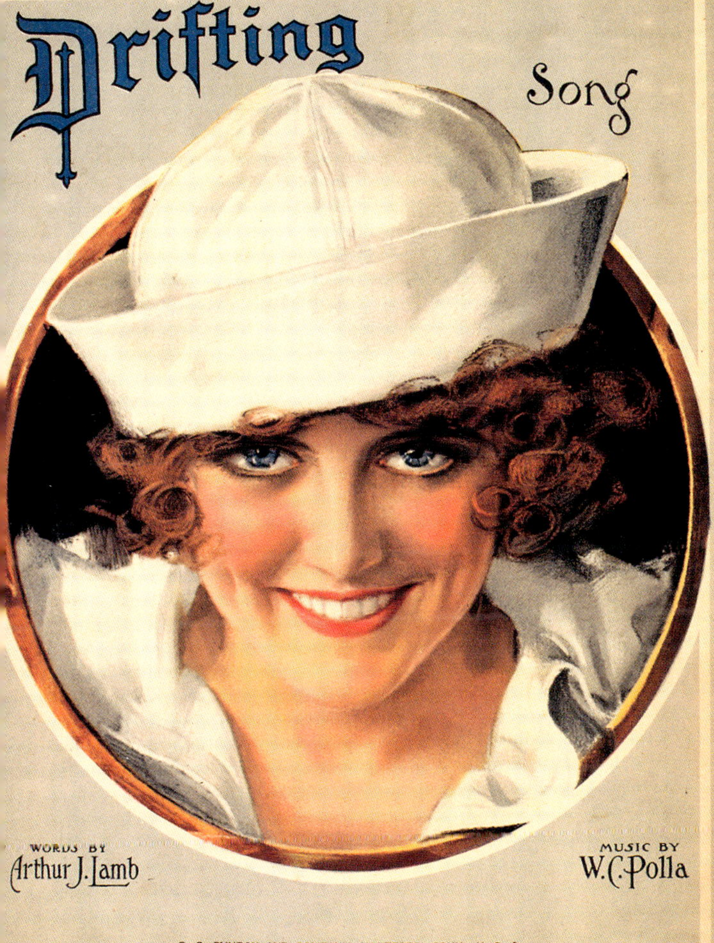

C. C. CHURCH AND COMPANY, HARTFORD, CONN., U. S. A.
HARTFORD NEW YORK LONDON PARIS SYDNEY

THE KNAPP CO., INC., N.Y.

$ .60
NET FR. 2.50

Knapp Co. Sheet Music
"There Must Be A Way To Love You"
1919

painted while he and Louise divided their time between Paris and the south of France. Little is known about his work in Paris; however, there is one known example of a nude rendered in oils by Armstrong. Under Armstrong's signature is lettered, "1921 Paris." Rolf and Louise returned to New York in 1921.

Rolf's work for tabloids, sheet music, and post cards declined in the mid-1920s, while new commissions emerged for magazine covers

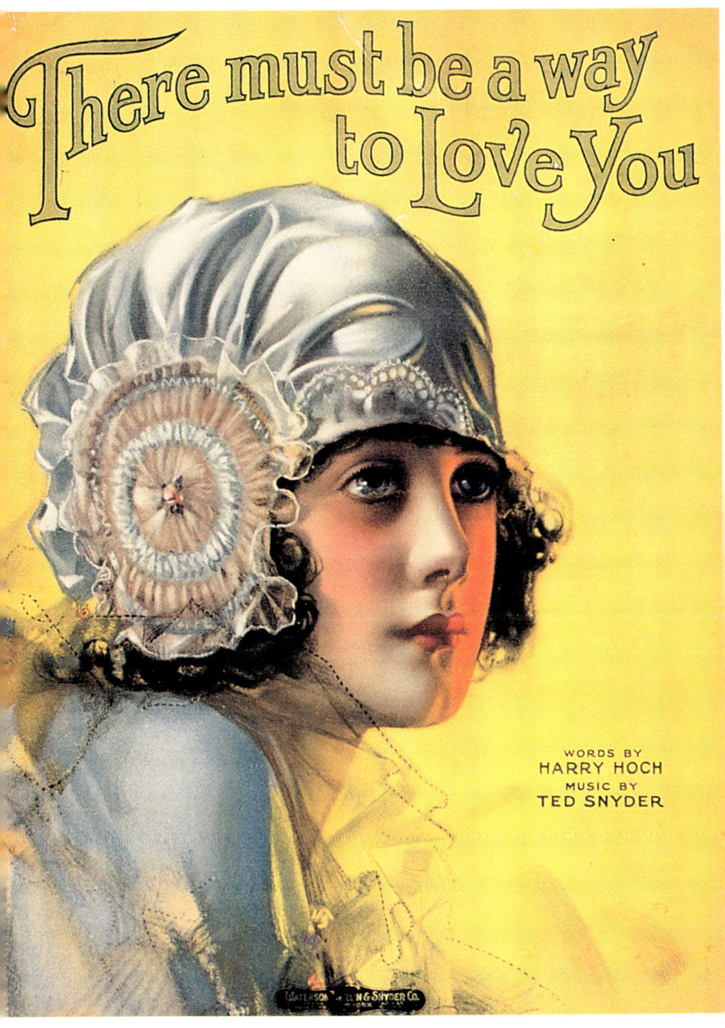
There must be a way to Love You
WORDS BY
HARRY HOCH
MUSIC BY
TED SNYDER
WATERSON
N & SNYDER CO.

Pictorial Review
Aug., 1925

(especially movie magazines), commercial advertising, private portraits, and calendars. Rolf became even more of a celebrity in the 1920s when commercial advertising suited his style very well. His prosperity prompted him to design and build a very unusual and imposing home on the shores of Little Neck Bay, Bayside, Long Island, New York.

It was during these Bayside years that Rolf undertook his grandest artistic endeavors. He began a series

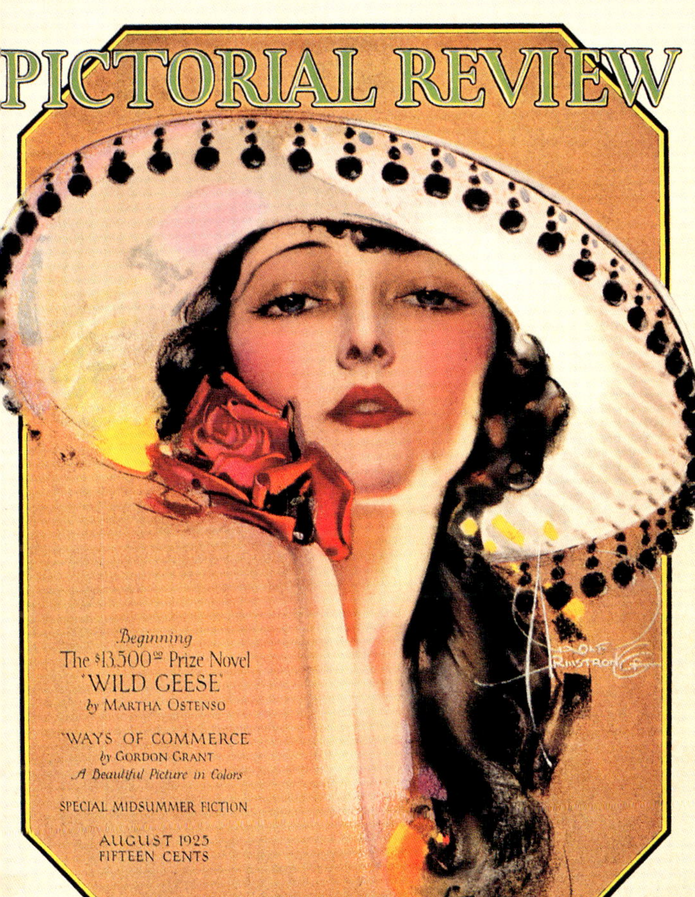
PICTORIAL REVIEW
Beginning
The $13,500.00 Prize Novel
"WILD GEESE"
by MARTHA OSTENSO
"WAYS OF COMMERCE"
by GORDON GRANT
A Beautiful Picture in Colors
SPECIAL MIDSUMMER FICTION
AUGUST 1925
FIFTEEN CENTS

The Shrine Magazine
Aug., 1928

of very large (sixty-by-eighty inch) oil paintings. His first, "Cleopatra" in 1924, was a phenomenal success. This painting appeared soon after the discovery of Pharaoh Tutankhamen's tomb and was the perfect calendar image for the time. Other great oil paintings were soon completed: "The Enchantress" in 1926; "Arabian Nights" in 1927; "Carmen" in 1929; and "Song of India" in 1930. All were added to Brown & Bigelow's impressive collection.

AUGUST 1928

The SHRINE MAGAZINE

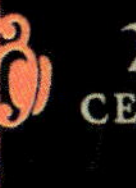

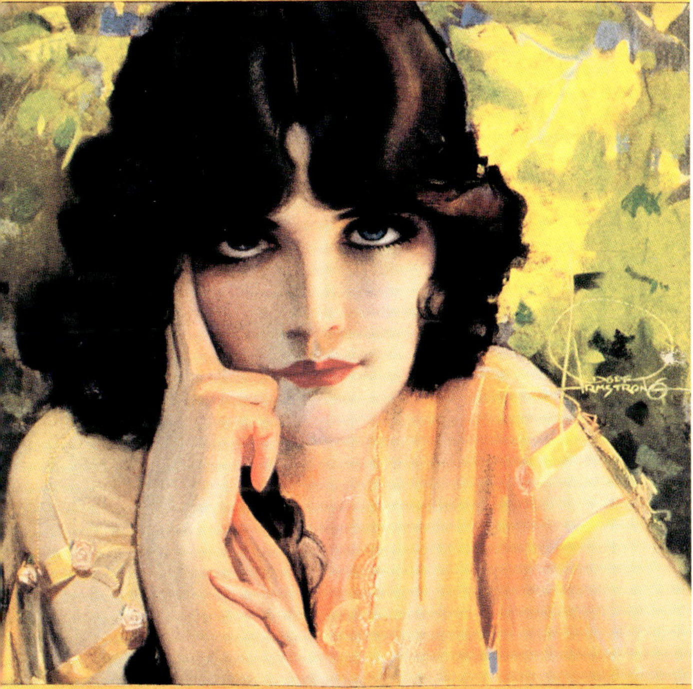

The STORM By F. BRITTEN AUSTIN

SNEEZERS & WHEEZERS by FRANK P. STOCKBRIDGE.

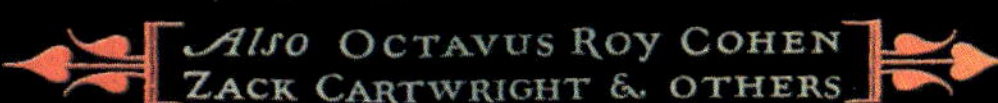

The Shrine Magazine
Oct., 1928

By 1927 executives at Brown & Bigelow considered Rolf Armstrong to be the leading American artist of beautiful women. Then he delivered "Dream Girl," executed in a exquisite and mysterious chiaroscuro style. This image, modeled by actress Anna Nilsson, soon positioned Rolf Armstrong as the undisputed king of feminine beauty within the calendar trade. Kissproof Cosmetics also used the image in their magazine advertising, and offered the print,

OCT. 1928

The SHRINE MAGAZINE

25 CENTS

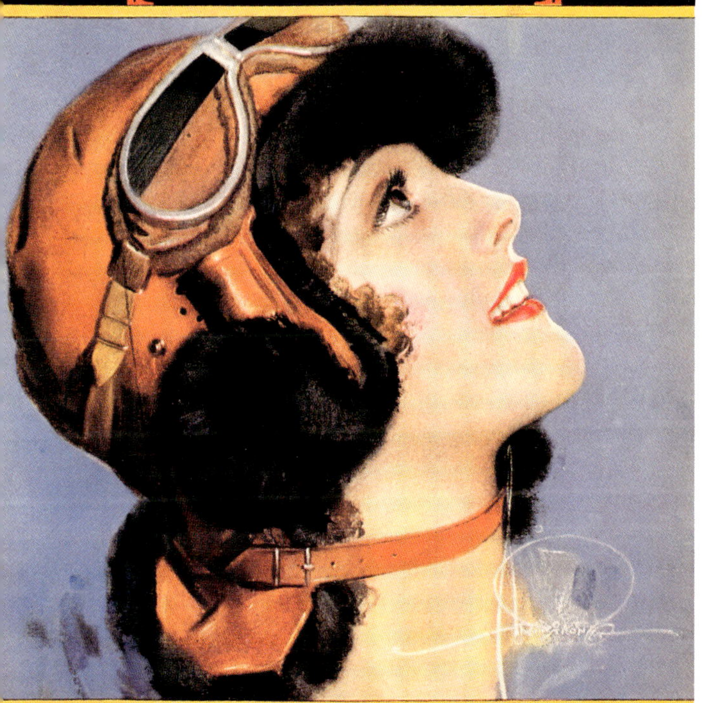

HALF SWORDS

A SERIAL OF FAMILY LIFE OF TO-DAY

By that Engaging Novelist *NALBRO BARTLEY*

WILLIAM ALMON WOLFF *INTERVIEWS* MARION TALLEY

FICTION & ARTICLES *by* ARTHUR STRINGER
FRANK P. STOCKBRIDGE & ZACK CARTWRIGHT

University "My Time Is Your Time"

Sep., 1933

renamed "The Kissproof Girl," as a premium. Twelve years later, in a 1940 *Life* magazine article about the popularity of calendar girl art, "Dream Girl" was again mentioned as the most commercially successful print of Brown & Bigelow's calendars.

By 1935 Rolf's nephew, Robert Armstrong, was an actor in Hollywood and had the male lead as Carl Denham in "King Kong." Rolf moved to Hollywood and built a new home and studio in an avocado grove in

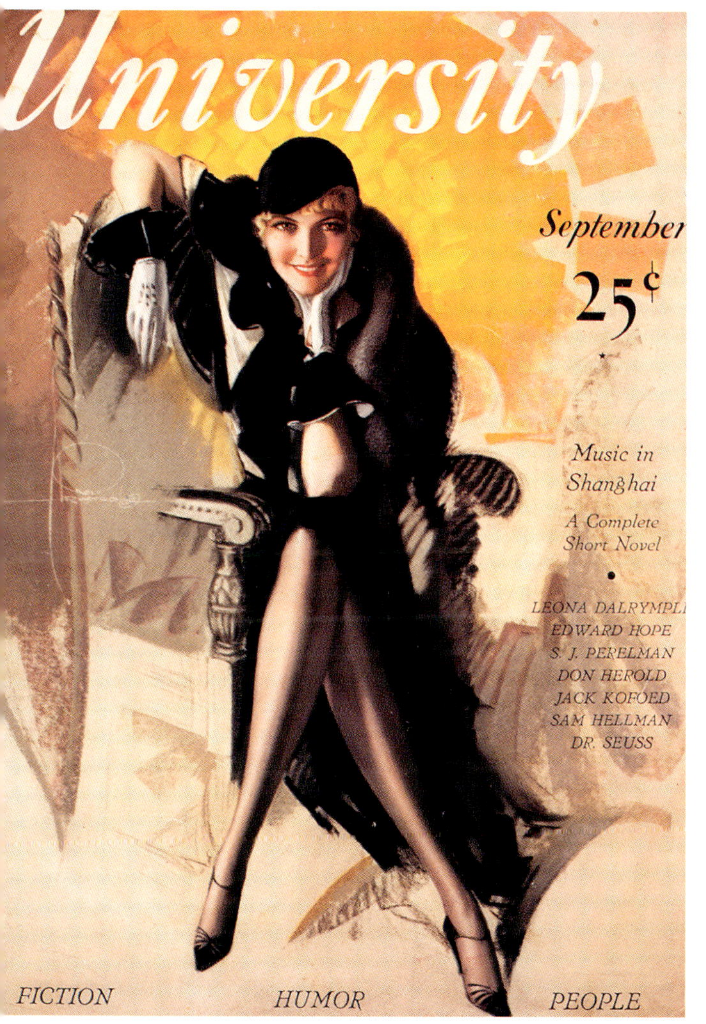
University
September
25¢
Music in
Shanghai
A Complete
Short Novel
LEONA DALRYMPL
EDWARD HOPE
S. J. PERELMAN
DON HEROLD
JACK KOFOED
SAM HELLMAN
DR. SEUSS
FICTION
HUMOR
PEOPLE

University
Nov., 1933

Coldwater Canyon. By now his work was so successful that he had two exhibits of his drawings, one in his studio and one in the Tennant Gallery on Sunset Boulevard. The second show included handsome portraits of Mrs. William Randolph Hearst, Marjorie Merriweather Post, Constance Bennett, James Gleason, and Boris Karloff as Frankenstein, as well as some sensitive studies of children.

Rolf's early paintings and drawings of women emphasized his

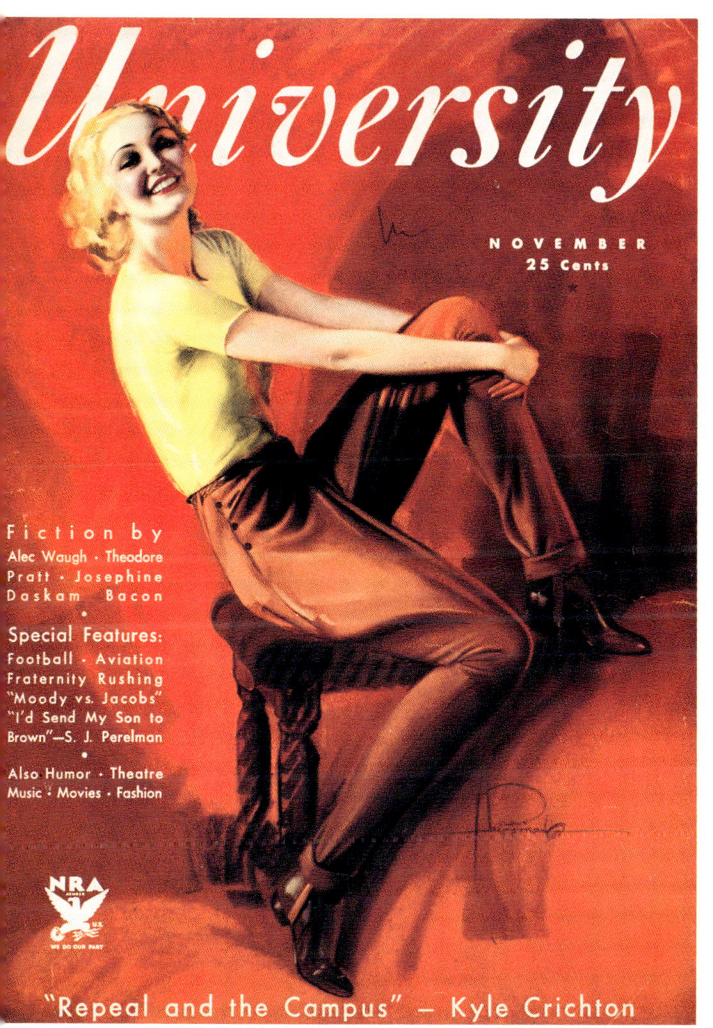
University
NOVEMBER
25 Cents
Fiction by
Alec Waugh · Theodore Pratt · Josephine Daskam Bacon
Special Features:
Football · Aviation
Fraternity Rushing
"Moody vs. Jacobs"
"I'd Send My Son to Brown"—S. J. Perelman
Also Humor · Theatre
Music · Movies · Fashion
NRA
WE DO OUR PART
"Repeal and the Campus" – Kyle Crichton

***Screenland* "Joan Crawford"**
June, 1930

ideals of youth, sweetness, and feminine charm. By the mid-1920s his work reflected more sophistication, maturity, and sometimes even a haughty deco look. These 1920s images of elegance and mystique have endured the tests of time, and are still today very appealing.

From the 1920s into the 1930s, Armstrong's vision of America's "Flapper Girl" reflected youthful charm. In 1930 Rolf hired New York City College student Dea Smith as a

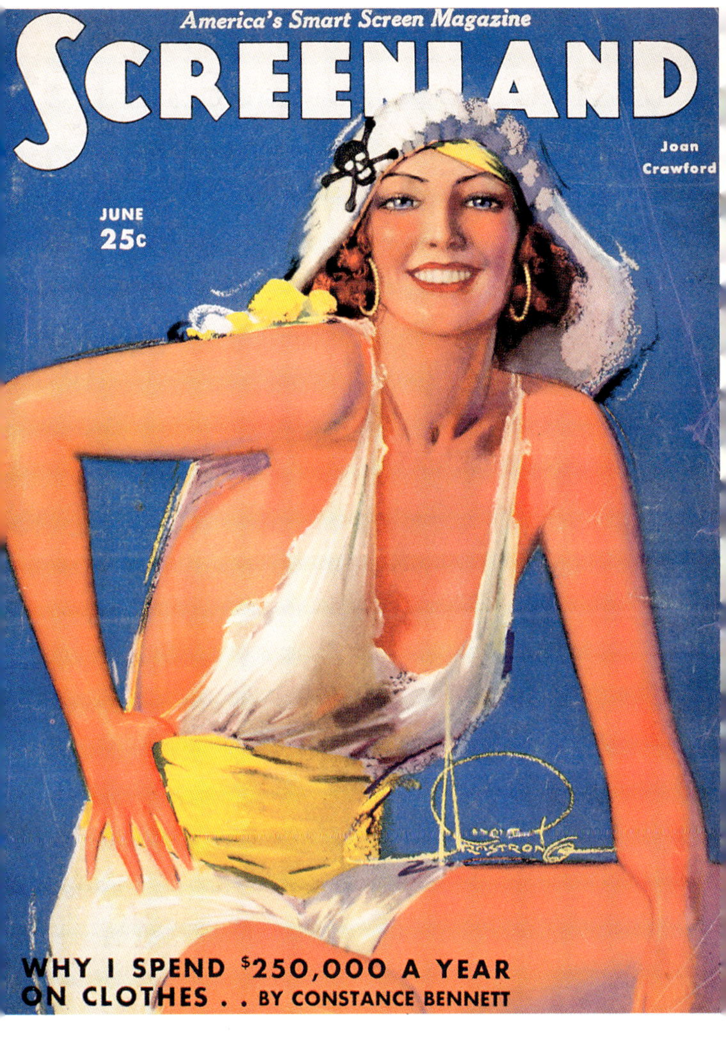
America's Smart Screen Magazine
SCREENLAND
Joan
Crawford
JUNE
25c
ARMSTRONG
WHY I SPEND $250,000 A YEAR
ON CLOTHES . . BY CONSTANCE BENNETT

Screenland "Anita Stewart"
May, 1924

model. She was soon a favorite model and began to appear on many *College Humor* covers, a popular college magazine of the era. Armstrong's illustrations were used by this publication from the mid-1920s for over a decade.

Unfortunately, the relationship between Rolf and Louise did not fare well during their Hollywood years. Their marriage ended in divorce on New Year's Eve 1938. Rolf must have felt that his life needed a new direction;

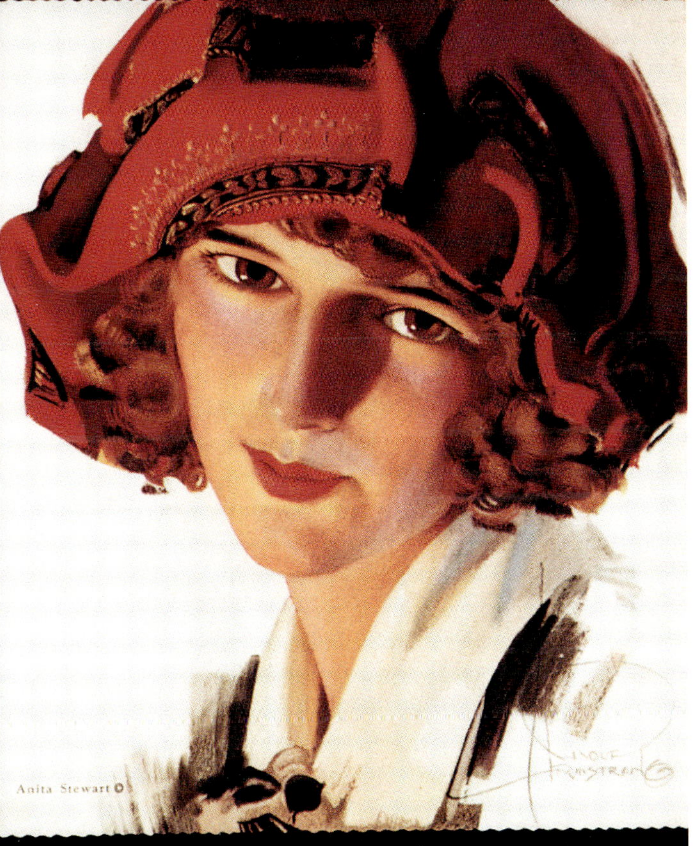
MAY 1924
PRICE 25 CENTS
SCREENLAND
Anita Stewart
The Jinx on Mabel Normand

Photoplay Magazine "Norma Talmadge"
Jan., 1920

so, late in 1939 he returned to the creative synergy of New York and moved into the famous Hotel Des Artistes in the heart of Manhattan. There he rented studio 614 and eventually, the coveted penthouse studio. Rolf was now home again. He loved New York, especially Manhattan, which he endearingly referred to as "Baghdad on the subway." From his penthouse deck he could enjoy the seasonal beauty of the "Magic Carpet," his pet name for Central Park.

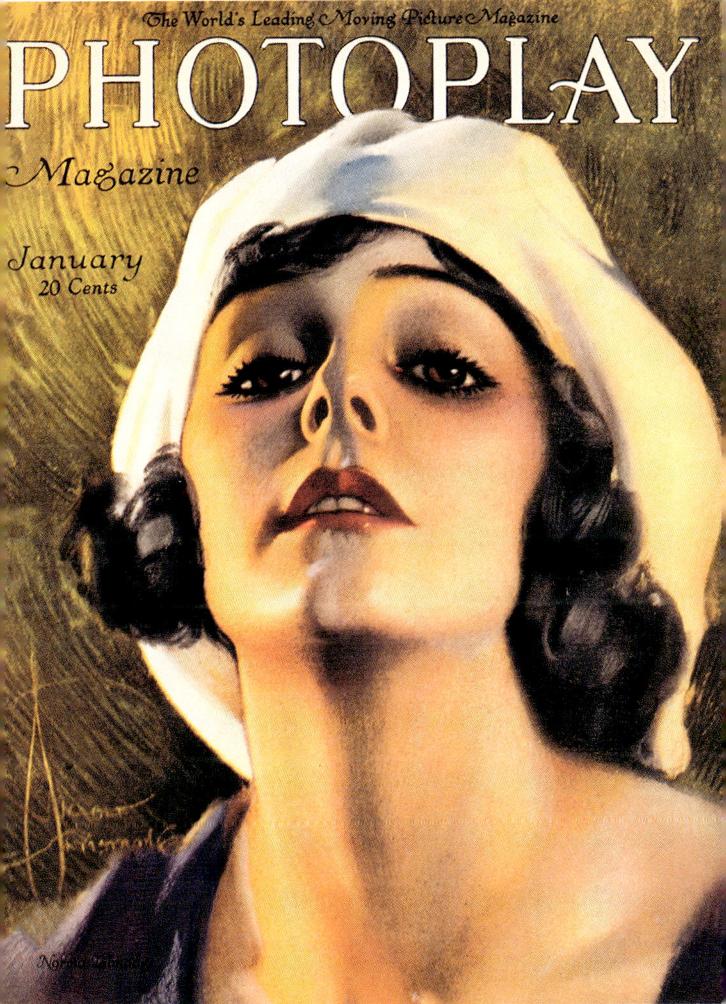
The World's Leading Moving Picture Magazine
PHOTOPLAY
Magazine
January
20 Cents

College Humor
Mar., 1927

For over two decades the "Armstrong Girls" appeared on the calendars of eight of America's calendar companies, both great and small. Brown & Bigelow, by far the giant among the group, had, since the 1920s, jealously and unsuccessfully pursued Armstrong for an exclusive contract. Finally in 1943, Charlie Ward, the forceful and determined president of Brown & Bigelow, persuaded Armstrong to sign a fifteen-year exclusive contract. Unless

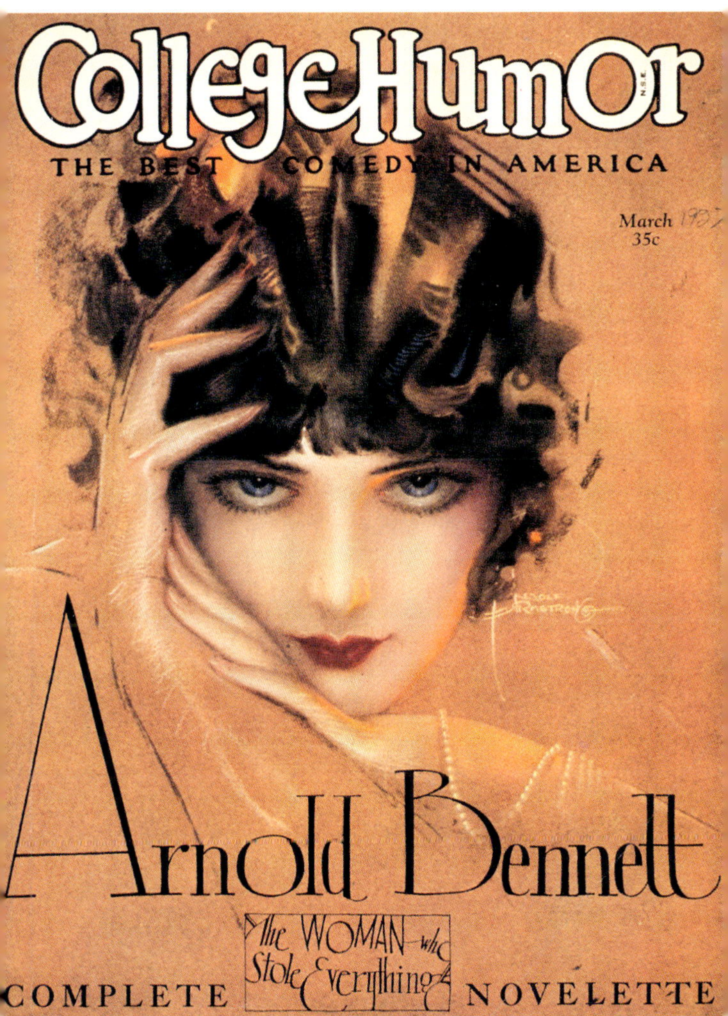
College Humor
N.S.E.
THE BEST COMEDY IN AMERICA
March
35c
Arnold Bennett
The WOMAN who Stole Everything
COMPLETE NOVELETTE

College Humor
Dec., 1927

permitted and sub-licensed by Brown & Bigelow, "Armstrong Girls" would appear only with their familiar trademark.

This was a busy and productive period for Armstrong. The nation was embroiled in World War II and the American calendar girl was a great morale booster both at home and abroad. Gone was the haughty look, for Rolf knew his "Armstrong Girl" should now reflect the sweetheart the G.I. left behind as he went to war. At

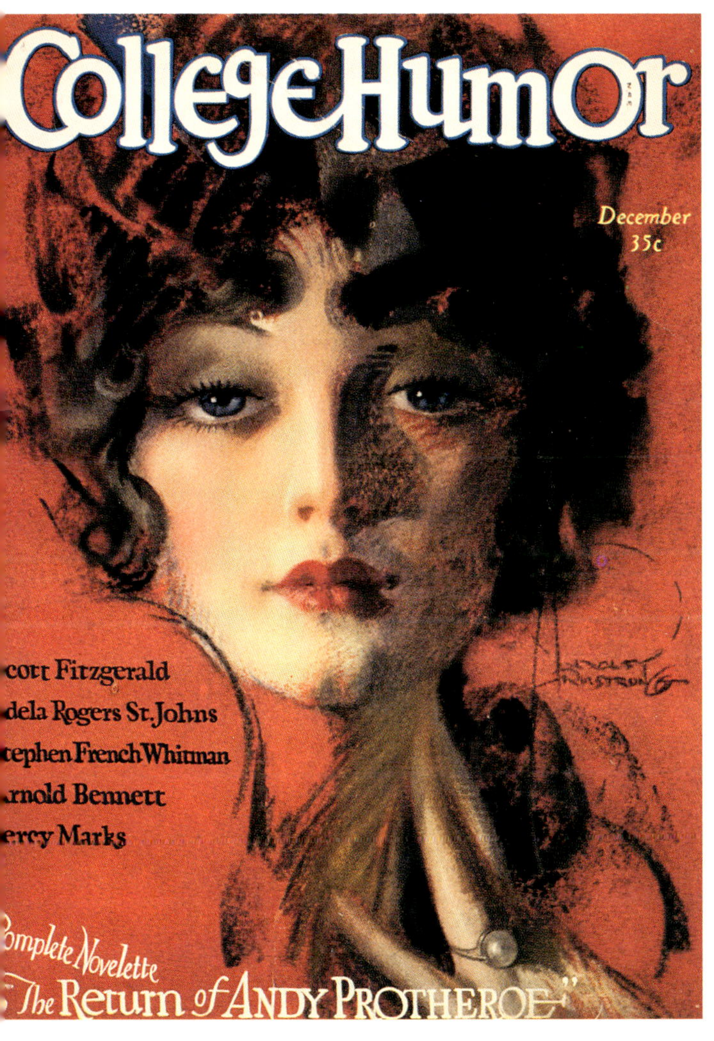
College Humor
December
35c
cott Fitzgerald
dela Rogers St. Johns
tephen French Whitman
rnold Bennett
ercy Marks
omplete Novelette
"The Return of Andy Protheroe"

College Humor
Dec., 1925

Brown & Bigelow, Rolf now competed with younger, very determined artists such as Zoe Mozert, Earl Moran, and Gil Elvgren. Then Rolf met and hired the beautiful and vivacious Miss Jewel Flowers and their first success revitalized his artistic interest. Their success so impressed Charlie Ward that he insisted Jewel also be under contract with Brown & Bigelow; she was the only artist's model to have that distinction. The successful working relationship continued throughout the

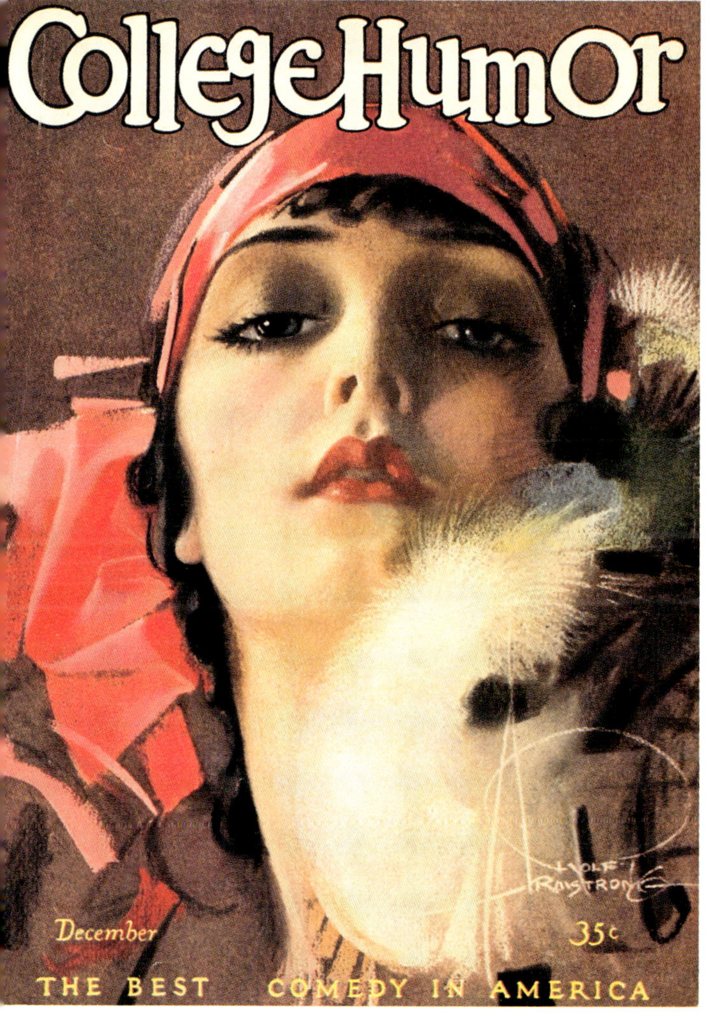
College Humor
ROLF ARMSTRONG
December
35c
THE BEST COMEDY IN AMERICA

College Humor
Feb., 1930

war and Jewel received hundreds of letters from U.S. servicemen. The flood of mail must have made a lasting impression on the local post office since a letter addressed simply to "Miss Jewel Flowers, New York City" was delivered.

With Jewel as inspiration, and the changing times, Rolf ventured into new themes for calendar images. Included with scenes of women supporting the war effort were images based on popular Latin dances which featured

College Humor

ALL-AMERICAN SELECTIONS

February
35c

im Tully
he Fitzgeralds
Iolworthy Hall
Morley Callaghan
Thyra Samter Winsl

"The College Club Murder" by Clifford Orr

College Humor
Mar., 1932

beautifully costumed and gowned women. The farmer's daughter working on the farm and western themes also became very popular. Moving into the 1940s and 1950s, the bikini girl became a popular "pin-up" theme.

Jewel remained Rolf's closest friend and confidante throughout his remaining years. She became his "Missy" and Rolf became her "Skipper." Their relationship was that of a caring father and fond daughter.

SMART HUMOR · BRIGHT COLORS · SUBTLE SATIRE

College Humor

MAY
35c

BEER
for the College Man & Eric Hatch's New Novel

College Humor
Jan., 1926

Jewel also had the honor and distinction of posing for the last Armstrong calendar. Following a tradition which lasted forty-two years, the final encore was in 1961 with "She's Tops," which was also Brown & Bigelow's farewell to the many years of showcasing their favorite and foremost creator of feminine beauty.

With fifteen years of contract deadlines and phenomenal success behind him, Rolf wanted to enjoy the fruits of his labors, and be creative

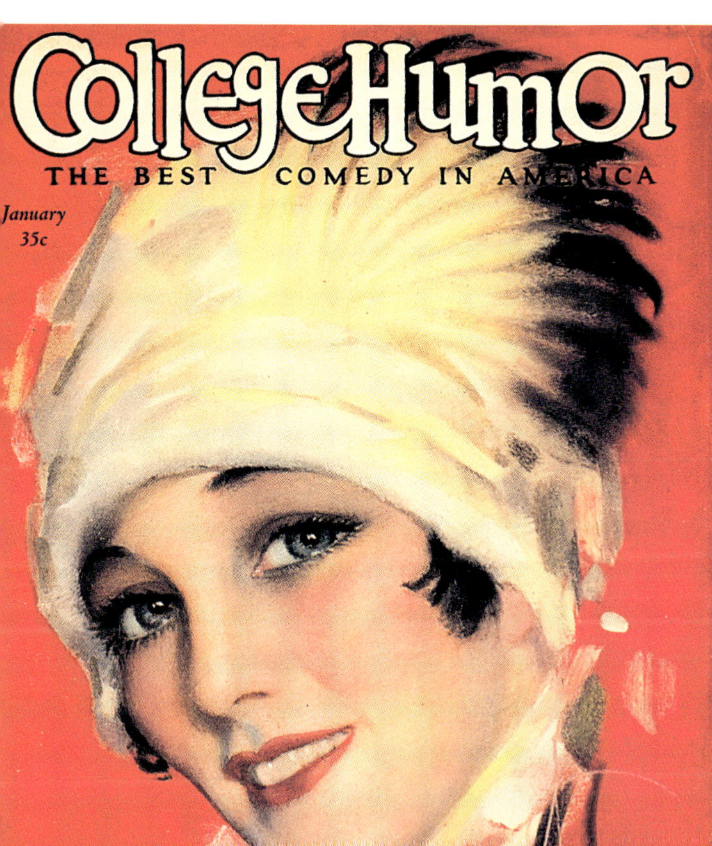

Lois Seyster Montross • Robert Benchley • Katharine Brush, Thyra Samter Winslow • John Held, Jr. • James Warner Bellah

College Humor "Double Beauty"
Apr., 1930

without the constant pressure. He enjoyed parties with many friends, who often included James Cagney and Henry Fonda (both who hammed it up with Rolf by singing and playing their ukuleles); comedian Harold Lloyd; two-time Olympic Gold Medalist Duke Kahanamoku; other noted artists; beautiful models; and his Missy, whenever he could borrow her from her duties as wife and mother. Often, Jewel was the hostess, and arranged all details to ensure that everyone

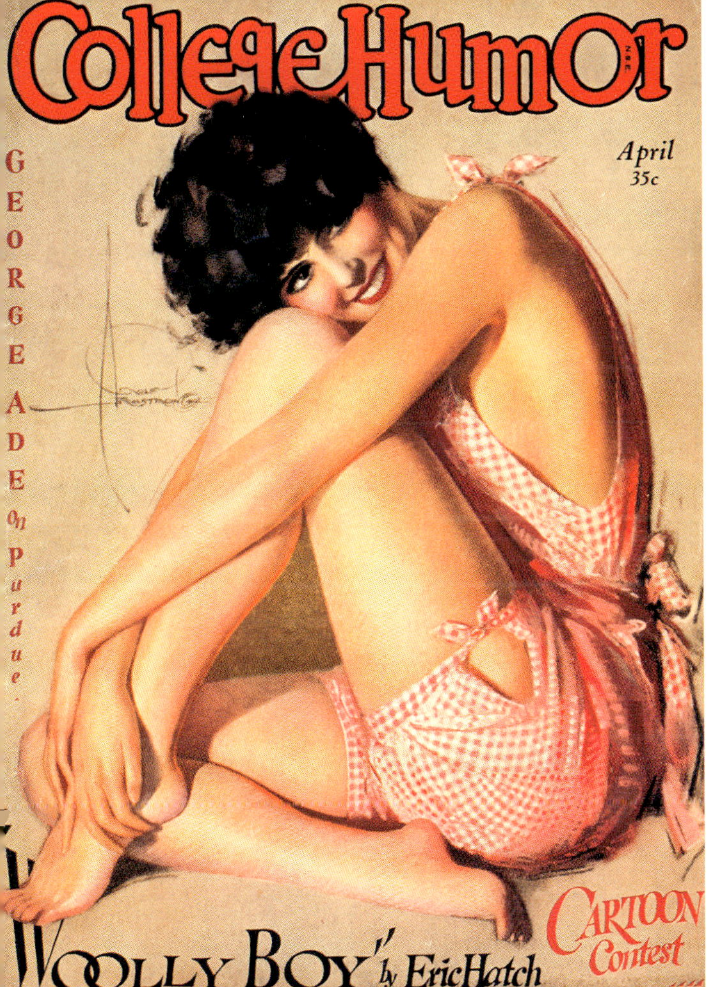
College Humor
April
35c
GEORGE ADE on Purdue.
"WOOLLY BOY" by Eric Hatch
CARTOON Contest

College Humor
Nov., 1932

enjoyed the party.

Rolf made several visits to the Hawaiian Islands during the 1950s. On a visit in 1952 he painted a beach scene with Elsa Edsman, the reigning Miss Hawaii. Elsa was featured on a Brown & Bigelow calendar in 1953 as "Sunny Skies."

Apparently the relaxed life style of the islands left its mark on Rolf. In September, 1959 Rolf moved to Waikiki, Honolulu, Hawaii, and

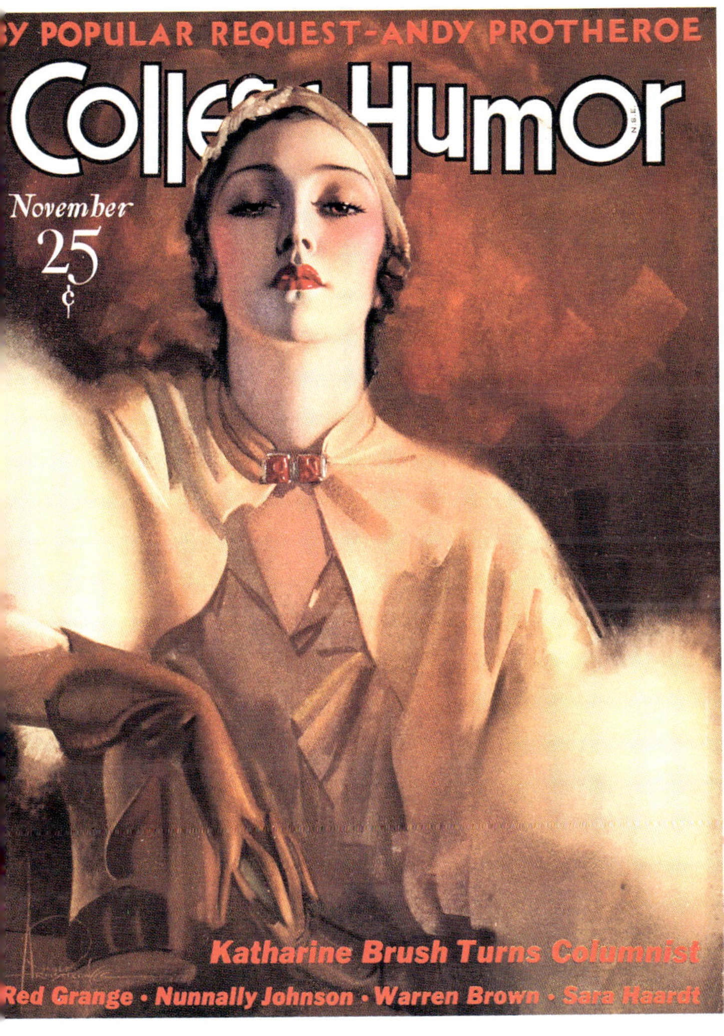

BY POPULAR REQUEST-ANDY PROTHEROE
College Humor
November
25¢
Katharine Brush Turns Columnist
Red Grange · Nunnally Johnson · Warren Brown · Sara Haardt

College Humor
Apr., 1927

retreated from the world of commercialism. He continued to draw, one of the remaining joys of his life. On November 11, 1959, Rolf suffered a slight stroke from which he apparently recovered. Sadly, just a few months later on February 22, 1960, he suffered a massive coronary thrombosis and died. Rolf's many friends on the mainland were overwhelmed by shock and grief. As he wished, his ashes were released into the trade winds

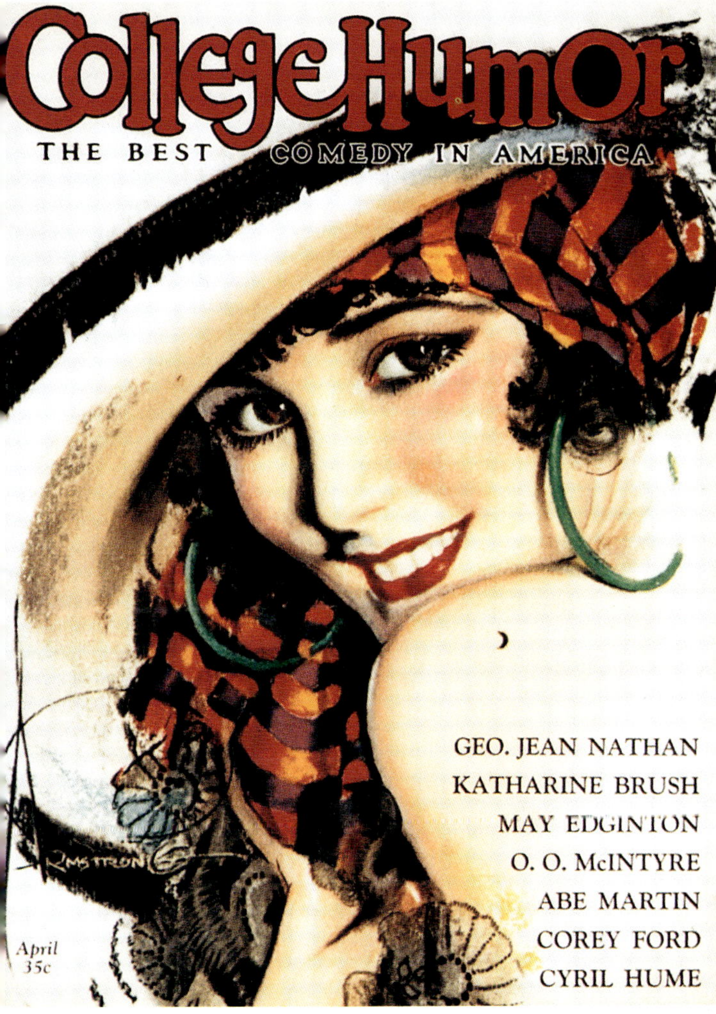
College Humor
THE BEST COMEDY IN AMERICA
GEO. JEAN NATHAN
KATHARINE BRUSH
MAY EDGINTON
O. O. McINTYRE
ABE MARTIN
COREY FORD
CYRIL HUME
April
35c

College Humor "Thinking of You"

Mar., 1932

from beautiful Mt. Pali over the Pali Pass on the island of Oahu. And there the "worshiper of beauty" became forever a part of beauty. Rolf is remembered most of all for his great love of life. Beauty and the essence of life called to him. To those lucky few who knew him well, it was this ingrained characteristic that endeared him to so many.

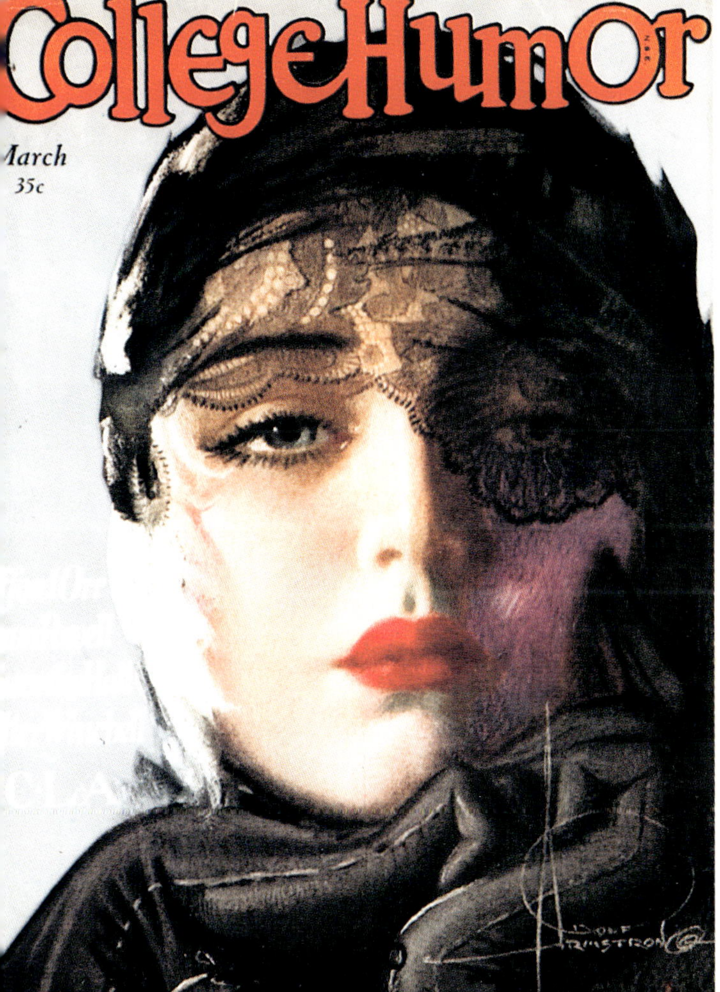
College Humor
March
35c

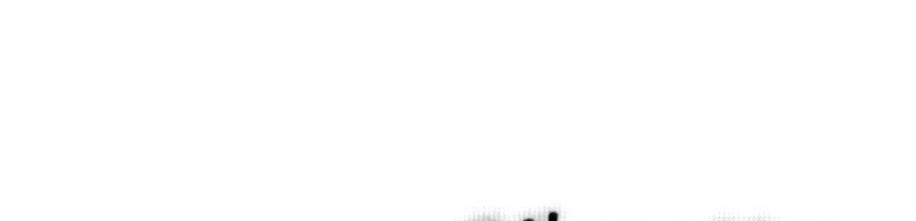

Vignettes